THE INCIDENT BOOK

THE
INCIDENT BOOK

*

FLEUR ADCOCK

Oxford   Auckland
OXFORD UNIVERSITY PRESS
1986

Oxford University Press, Walton Street, Oxford OX2 6DP
Oxford New York Toronto
Delhi Bombay Calcutta Madras Karachi
Petaling Jaya Singapore Hong Kong Tokyo
Nairobi Dar es Salaam Cape Town
Melbourne Auckland
and associated companies in
Beirut Berlin Ibadan Nicosia

Oxford is a trade mark of Oxford University Press

British Library Cataloguing in Publication Data
Adcock, Fleur
The incident book.
I. Title
821   PR9639.2.A/
ISBN 0-19-282029-X

Typeset by Joshua Associates Limited, Oxford
Printed in Great Britain by
J. W. Arrowsmith Ltd., Bristol

For my god-daughter, Heidi Jackson,
and in memory of her mother, Pauline

ACKNOWLEDGEMENTS

Poems from this collection have appeared in: *Ambit*, *Bananas*, *Country Life*, *Island Magazine*, *Landfall*, the *London Review of Books*, the *New Statesman*, the *New Zealand Listener*, *Oxford Poetry*, *Poetry Australia*, *Poetry Book Society Supplements* 1982, 1984, and 1985, *Poetry Review*, and the *Times Literary Supplement*.

Several poems have been broadcast by the BBC in *Poetry Now* and *The Living Poet*.

'Street Scene, London N2' was commissioned by the BBC for *English by Radio*.

'Leaving the Tate' was commissioned by the Tate Gallery.

CONTENTS

SCHOOLS

TELLING TALES

INCIDENTALS

THATCHERLAND

Uniunea Scriitorilor

Caterpillars are falling on the Writers' Union.
The writers are indifferent to the caterpillars.
They sit over their wine at the metal tables
wearing animated expressions and eating fried eggs
with pickled gherkins, or, (the dish of the day),
extremely small sausages: two each.

Meanwhile here and there an inch of grey bristles,
a miniature bottle-brush, twitches along a sleeve
or clings to a shoulder. The stone-paved courtyard
is dappled with desperate clumps of whiskers,
launched from the sunlit mulberry trees
to take their chance among literary furniture.

A poet ignores a fluffy intruder
in his bread-basket (the bread's all finished)
but flicks another from the velvet hat
(which surely she must have designed herself—
such elegance never appears in the shop-windows)
of his pretty companion, who looks like an actress.

The writers are talking more and more rapidly.
Not all are writers. One is a painter;
many are translators. Even those who are not
are adaptable and resourceful linguists.
'Pardon!' says one to the foreign visitor.
'Permit me! You have a worm on your back.'

Leaving the Tate

Coming out with your clutch of postcards
in a Tate Gallery bag and another clutch
of images packed into your head you pause
on the steps to look across the river

and there's a new one: light bright buildings,
a streak of brown water, and such a sky
you wonder who painted it—Constable? No:
too brilliant. Crome? No: too ecstatic—

a madly pure Pre-Raphaelite sky,
perhaps, sheer blue apart from the white plumes
rushing up it (today, that is,
April. Another day would be different

but it wouldn't matter. All skies work.)
Cut to the lower right for a detail:
seagulls pecking on mud, below
two office blocks and a Georgian terrace.

Now swing to the left, and take in plane-trees
bobbled with seeds, and that brick building,
and a red bus . . . Cut it off just there,
by the lamp-post. Leave the scaffolding in.

That's your next one. Curious how
these outdoor pictures didn't exist
before you'd looked at the indoor pictures,
the ones on the walls. But here they are now,

marching out of their panorama
and queuing up for the viewfinder
your eye's become. You can isolate them
by holding your optic muscles still.

You can zoom in on figure studies
(that boy with the rucksack), or still lives,

abstracts, townscapes. No one made them.
The light painted them. You're in charge

of the hanging committee. Put what space
you like around the ones you fix on,
and gloat. Art multiplies itself.
Art's whatever you choose to frame.

The Bedroom Window

A small dazzle of stained glass which
I did not choose but might have, hanging
in front of the branches of a pine tree
which I do not own but covet; beyond them
a view of crinkly hills which I do not
etc and did not etc but might have
in another life, or the same life earlier.

The cat is fed, the plants are watered,
the milkman will call; the pine tree smells like
childhood. I am pretending to live here.
Out beyond the coloured glass and
the window-glass and the gully tall with
pine trees I dive back to wherever
I got my appetite for hills from.

The Chiffonier

You're glad I like the chiffonier. But I
feel suddenly uneasy, scenting why
you're pleased I like this pretty thing you've bought,
the twin of one that stood beside your cot
when you were small: you've marked it down for me;
it's not too heavy to be sent by sea
when the time comes, and it's got space inside
to pack some other things you've set aside,
things that are small enough to go by water
twelve thousand miles to me, your English daughter.
I know your habits—writing all our names
in books and on the backs of picture-frames,
allotting antique glass and porcelain dishes
to granddaughters according to their wishes,
promising me the tinted photograph
of my great-grandmother. We used to laugh,
seeing how each occasional acquisition
was less for you than for later disposition:
'You know how Marilyn likes blue and white
china? I've seen some plates I thought I might
indulge in.' Bless you, Mother! But we're not
quite so inclined to laugh now that you've got
something that's new to you but not a part
of your estate: that weakness in your heart.
It makes my distance from you, when I go
back home next week, suddenly swell and grow
from thirty hours' flying to a vast
galactic space between present and past.
How many more times can I hope to come
to Wellington and find you still at home?
We've talked about it, as one has to, trying
to see the lighter aspects of your dying:
'You've got another twenty years or more'
I said, 'but when you think you're at death's door
just let me know. I'll come and hang about
for however long it takes to see you out.'
'I don't think it'll be like that' you said:
'I'll pop off suddenly one night in bed.'

5

How secretive! How satisfying! You'll
sneak off, a kid running away from school—
well, that at least's the only way I find
I can bring myself to see it in my mind.
But now I see you in your Indian skirt
and casual cornflower-blue linen shirt
in the garden, under your feijoa tree,
looking about as old or young as me.
Dear little Mother! Naturally I'm glad
you found a piece of furniture that had
happy associations with your youth;
and yes, I do admire it—that's the truth:
its polished wood and touch of Art Nouveau
appeal to me. But surely you must know
I value this or any other treasure
of yours chiefly because it gives you pleasure.
I have to write this now, while you're still here:
I want my mother, not her chiffonier.

Tadpoles

For Oliver

Their little black thread legs, their threads of arms,
their mini-miniature shoulders, elbows, knees—
this piquant angularity, delicious
after that rippling smoothness, after nothing
but a flow of curves and roundnesses in water;
and their little hands, the size of their hands, the fingers
like hair-stubble, and their clumps-of-eyelashes feet . . .

Taddies, accept me as your grandmother,
a hugely gloating grand-maternal frog,
almost as entranced by other people's
tadpoles as I once was by my own,
that year when Oliver was still a tadpole
in Elizabeth's womb, and I a grandmother
only prospectively, and at long distance.

All this glory from globes of slithery glup!
Well, slithery glup was all right, with its cloudy
compacted spheres, its polka dots of blackness.
Then dots evolved into commas; the commas hatched.
When they were nothing but animated match-heads
with tails, a flickering flock of magnified
spermatazoa, they were already my darlings.

And Oliver lay lodged in his dreamy sphere,
a pink tadpole, a promise of limbs and language,
while my avatars of infancy grew up
into ribbon-tailed black-currants, fluttery-smooth,
and then into soaked brown raisins, a little venous,
with touches of transparency at the sides
where limbs minutely hinted at themselves.

It is the transformation that enchants.
As a mother reads her child's form in the womb,
imaging eyes and fingers, radar-sensing
.a thumb in a blind mouth, so tadpole-watchers

7

can stare at the cunning shapes beneath the skin
and await the tiny, magnificent effloration.
It is a lesson for a grandmother.

My tadpoles grew to frogs in their generation;
they may have been the grandparents of these
about-to-be frogs. And Oliver's a boy,
hopping and bouncing in his bright green tracksuit,
my true darling; but too far away now
for me to call him across the world and say
'Oliver, look at what's happening to the tadpoles!'

For Heidi with Blue Hair

When you dyed your hair blue
(or, at least, ultramarine
for the clipped sides, with a crest
of jet-black spikes on top)
you were sent home from school

because, as the headmistress put it,
·although dyed hair was not
specifically forbidden, yours
was, apart from anything else,
not done in the school colours.

Tears in the kitchen, telephone-calls
to school from your freedom-loving father:
'She's not a punk in her behaviour;
it's just a style.' (You wiped your eyes,
also not in a school colour.)

'She discussed it with me first—
we checked the rules.' 'And anyway, Dad,
it cost twenty-five dollars.
Tell them it won't wash out—
not even if I wanted to try.'

It would have been unfair to mention
your mother's death, but that
shimmered behind the arguments.
The school had nothing else against you;
the teachers twittered and gave in.

Next day your black friend had hers done
in grey, white and flaxen yellow—
the school colours precisely:
an act of solidarity, a witty
tease. The battle was already won.

The Keepsake

In memory of Pete Laver

'To Fleur from Pete, on loan perpetual.'
It's written on the flyleaf of the book
I wouldn't let you give away outright:
'Just make it permanent loan' I said—a joke
between librarians, professional
jargon. It seemed quite witty, on a night

when most things passed for wit. We were all hoarse
by then, from laughing at the bits you'd read
aloud—the heaving bosoms, blushing sighs,
demoniac lips. 'Listen to this!' you said:
' "Thus rendered bold by frequent intercourse
I dared to take her hand." ' We wiped our eyes.

' "Colonel, what mean these stains upon your dress?" '
We howled. And then there was Lord Ravenstone
faced with Augusta's dutiful rejection
in anguished prose; or, for a change of tone,
a touch of Gothic: Madame la Comtesse
's walled-up lover. An inspired collection:

The Keepsake, 1835; the standard
drawing-room annual, useful as a means
for luring ladies into chaste flirtation
in early 19th century courtship scenes.
I'd never seen a copy; often wondered.
Well, here it was—a pretty compilation

of tales and verses: stanzas by Lord Blank
and Countess This and Mrs That; demure
engravings, all white shoulders, corkscrew hair
and swelling bosoms; stories full of pure
sentiments, in which gentlemen of rank
urged suits upon the nobly-minded fair.

You passed the volume round, and poured more wine.
Outside your cottage lightning flashed again:
a Grasmere storm, theatrically right
for stories of romance and terror. Then
somehow, quite suddenly, the book was mine.
The date in it's five weeks ago tonight.

'On loan perpetual.' If that implied
some dark finality, some hint of 'nox
perpetua', something desolate and bleak,
we didn't see it then, among the jokes.
Yesterday, walking on the fells, you died.
I'm left with this, a trifling, quaint antique.

You'll not reclaim it now; it's mine to keep:
a keepsake, nothing more. You've changed the 'loan
perpetual' to a bequest by dying.
Augusta, Lady Blanche, Lord Ravenstone—
I've read the lot, trying to get to sleep.
The jokes have all gone flat. I can't stop crying.

England's Glory

Red-tipped, explosive, self-complete:
one you can strike on the coal-face, or
the sole of your boot. Not for the south, where
soft men with soft hands rub effete
brown-capped sticks on a toning strip
chequered with coffee-grounds, the only
match for the matches, and any lonely
stray (if they let them stray) picked up
from a table or found loose in a pocket
can't, without its container, flare
fire at a stroke: is not a pure-
ly self-contained ignition unit.

'Security' proclaims the craven
yellow box with its Noah's ark,
'Brymay' Special Safety's trade-mark
for southern consumption. That's all right, then:
bankers can take them home to Surrey
for their cigars, and scatter the odd
match-head, whether or not it's dead,
on their parquet floors, without the worry
of subsequent arson. Not like here
where a match is a man's match, an object
to be handled with as much respect
but as casually as a man's beer.

You can't mistake the England's Glory
box: its crimson, blue and white
front's a miniature banner, fit
for the Durham Miners' Gala, gaudy
enough to march ahead of a band.
Forget that placid ark: the vessel
this one's adorned with has two funnels
gushing fat blue smoke to the wind.
The side's of sandpaper. The back
label's functional, printed with either
holiday vouchers, a special offer
on World Cup tickets, or this month's joke.

Somewhere across England's broad
midriff, wanderingly drawn
from west to east, there exists a line
to the north of which the shops provide
(catering for a sudden switch
of taste) superior fried fish, runnier
yogurt, blouses cut for the fuller
northern figure; and the northern match.
Here England's Glory begins; through all
the vigorous north it reigns unrivalled
until its truce with Scottish Bluebell
round about Berwick and Carlisle.

The Genius of Surrey

The landscape of my middle childhood
lacked factories. There had been no
industrial revolution in Surrey,
was the message. Woods and shops and houses,
churches, allotments, pubs and schools
and loonie-bins were all we had.

Except, of course, the sewerage works,
on 'Surridge Hill', as we used to call it.
How sweetly rural the name sounds!
Wordsworth's genius, said Walter Pater,
would have found its true test
had he become the poet of Surrey.

Yorkshire had a talent for mills
and placed them to set off its contours;
Westmorland could also have worn
a few more factories with an air.
As for Surrey's genius, that
was found to be for the suburban.

Loving Hitler

There they were around the wireless
waiting to listen to Lord Haw-Haw.
'Quiet now, children!' they said as usual:
'Ssh, be quiet! We're trying to listen.'
'Germany calling!' said Lord Haw-Haw.

I came out with it: 'I love Hitler.'
They turned on me: 'You can't love *Hitler*!
Dreadful, wicked—' (mutter, mutter,
the shocked voices buzzing together)—
'Don't be silly. You don't mean it.'

I held out for perhaps five minutes,
a mini-proto-neo-Nazi,
six years old and wanting attention.
Hitler always got their attention;
now I had it, for five minutes.

Everyone at school loved someone,
and it had to be a boy or a man
if you were a girl. So why not Hitler?
Of course, you couldn't love Lord Haw-Haw;
but Hitler—well, he was so famous!

It might be easier to love Albert,
the boy who came to help with the milking,
but Albert laughed at me. Hitler wouldn't:
one thing you could say for Hitler,
you never heard him laugh at people.

All the same, I settled for Albert.

SCHOOLS

Halfway Street, Sidcup

'We did sums at school, Mummy—
you do them like this: look.' I showed her.

It turned out she knew already.

St Gertrude's, Sidcup

Nuns, now: ladies in black hoods
for teachers—surely that was surprising?

It seems not. It was just England:
like houses made of brick, with stairs,

and dark skies, and Christmas coming
in winter, and there being a war on.

I was five, and unsurprisable—
except by nasty dogs, or the time

when I ran to catch the bus from school
and my knickers fell down in the snow.

Scalford School

The French boy was sick on the floor at prayers.
For years his name made me feel sick too:
Maurice. The teachers said it the English way,
but he was French, or French-speaking—
Belgian, perhaps; at any rate from some

country where things were wrong in 1940.
Until I grew up, 'Maurice' meant
his narrow pale face, pointed chin,
bony legs, and the wet pink sick.

But we were foreign too, of course,
my sister and I, in spite of our
unthinkingly acquired Leicestershire accents.
An older girl was struck one day
by our, to us, quite ordinary noses;
made an anthropological deduction:
'Have all the other people in New Zealand
got silly little noses too?'
I couldn't remember. Firmly I said 'Yes.'

Salfords, Surrey

Forget about the school—there was one,
which I've near enough forgotten.

But look at this—and you still can,
on the corner of Honeycrock Lane—

this tiny tin-roofed shed of brick,
once the smallest possible Public

Library. I used to lie
flat on the floor, and work my way

along the shelves, trying to choose
between Rose Fyleman's fairy verse

and *Tales of Sir Benjamin Bulbous, Bart*.
The book that really stuck in my heart

I can't identify: a saga
about a talking horse, the Pooka,

and Kathleen, and the quest they both
made through tunnels under the earth

for—something. Herbs and flowers came
into it, spangled through a dream

of eyebright, speedwell, Kathleen's bare
legs blotched blue with cold. Well; there

were other stories. When I'd read
all mine I'd see what Mummy had.

Of Mice and Men: that sounded nice.
I'd just got far enough to notice

it wasn't much like *Peter Rabbit*
when she took it away and hid it.

No loss, I'd say. But where shall I find
the Pooka's travels underground?

Outwood

Milkmaids, buttercups, ox-eye daisies,
white and yellow in the tall grass:
I fought my way to school through flowers—
bird's-foot trefoil, clover, vetch—
my sandals all smudged with pollen,
seedy grass-heads caught in my socks.

At school I used to read, mostly,
and hide in the shed at dinnertime,
writing poems in my notebook.
'Little fairies dancing', I wrote,
and 'Peter and I, we watch the birds fly,
high in the sky, in the evening.'

Then home across the warm common
to tease my little sister again:
'I suppose you thought I'd been to school:
I've been to work in a bicycle shop.'
Mummy went to a real job
every day, on a real bicycle;

Doris used to look after us.
She took us for a walk with a soldier,
through the damp ferns in the wood
into a clearing like a garden,
rosy-pink with beds of campion,
herb-robert, lady's smock.

The blackberry briars were pale with blossom.
I snagged my tussore dress on a thorn;
Doris didn't even notice.
She and the soldier lay on the grass;
he leaned over her pink blouse
and their voices went soft and round, like petals.

On the School Bus

The little girls in the velvet collars
(twins, we thought) had lost their mother:
the ambulance men had had to scrape her
off the road, said the sickening whispers.

Horror's catching. The safe procedure
to ward it off, or so we gathered,
was a homeopathic dose of torture.
So we pulled their hair, like all the others.

Earlswood

Air-raid shelters at school were damp tunnels
where you sang 'Ten Green Bottles' yet again
and might as well have been doing decimals.

At home, though, it was cosier and more fun:
cocoa and toast inside the Table Shelter,
our iron-panelled bunker, our new den.

By day we ate off it; at night you'd find us
under it, the floor plump with mattresses
and the wire grilles neatly latched around us.

You had to be careful not to bump your head;
we padded the hard metal bits with pillows,
then giggled in our glorious social bed.

What could be safer? What could be more romantic
than playing cards by torchlight in a raid?
Odd that it made our mother so neurotic

to hear the sirens; we were quite content—
but slightly cramped once there were four of us,
after we'd taken in old Mrs Brent

from down by the Nag's Head, who'd been bombed out.
She had her arm in plaster, but she managed
to dress herself, and smiled, and seemed all right.

Perhaps I just imagined hearing her
moaning a little in the night, and shaking
splinters of glass out of her long grey hair.

The next week we were sent to Leicestershire.

Scalford Again

Being in Mr Wood's class this time,
and understanding, when he explained it clearly,
about the outside of a bicycle wheel
travelling around faster than the centre;
and not minding his warts; and liking Scripture
because of the Psalms: I basked in all this
no less than in the Infants the time before,

with tambourines and Milly-Molly-Mandy.
Although I'd enjoyed Milly-Molly-Mandy:
it had something to do with apricots, I thought,
or marigolds; or some warm orange glow.

Neston

Just visiting: another village school
with a desk for me to fill, while Chippenham
decided whether it wanted me—too young
for there, too over-qualified for here.

I knew it all—except, of course, geography.
Here was a map; I vaguely scratched in towns.
Ah, but here was a job: the infant teacher
was called away for half an hour. Would I . . . ?

Marooned there in a tide of little bodies
alive with Wiltshire voices, I was dumb.
They skipped about my feet, a flock of lambs
bleating around a daft young heifer.

Chippenham

The maths master was eight feet tall.
He jabbed his clothes'-prop arm at me
halfway across the classroom, stretched
his knobbly finger, shouted 'You!

You're only here one day in three,
and when you are you might as well
not be, for all the work you do!
What do you think you're playing at?'

What did I think? I shrank into
my grubby blouse. Who did I think
I was, among these blazered boys,
these tidy girls in olive serge?

My green skirt wasn't uniform:
clothes were on coupons, after all.
I'd get a gymslip—blue, not green—
for Redhill Grammar, some time soon

when we went home. But, just for now,
what did I think? I thought I was
betrayed. I thought of how I'd stood
an hour waiting for the bus

that morning, by a flooded field,
watching the grass-blades drift and sway
beneath the water like wet hair;
hoping for Mrs Johnson's call:

'Jean, are you there? The clock was wrong.
You've missed the bus.' And back I'd run
to change my clothes, be Jean again,
play with the baby, carry pails

of water from the village tap,
go to the shop, eat toast and jam,
and then, if she could shake enough
pennies and farthings from her bag,

we might get to the pictures. But
the clock was fast, it seemed, not slow;
the bus arrived; and as I slid
anonymously into it

an elegant male prefect said
'Let Fleur sit down, she's got bad feet.'
I felt my impetigo scabs
blaze through my shoes. How did he know?

23

Tunbridge Wells

My turn for Audrey Pomegranate,
all-purpose friend for newcomers;
the rest had had enough of her—
her too-much hair, her too-much flesh,
her moles, her sideways-gliding mouth,
her smirking knowledge about rabbits.

Better a gluey friend than none,
and who was I to pick and choose?
She nearly stuck; but just in time
I met a girl called Mary Button,
a neat Dutch doll as clean as soap,
and Audrey P. was back on offer.

The High Tree

There was a tree higher than clouds or lightning,
higher than any plane could fly.

England huddled under its roots; leaves from it
fluttered on Europe out of the sky.

The weather missed it: it was higher than weather,
up in the sunshine, always dry.

It was a refuge. When you sat in its branches
threatening strangers passed you by.

Nothing could find you. Even friendly people,
if you invited them to try,

couldn't climb very far. It made them dizzy:
they'd shiver and shut their eyes and cry,

and you'd have to guide them down again, backwards,
wishing they hadn't climbed so high.

So it wasn't a social tree. It was perfect
for someone solitary and shy

who liked gazing out over miles of history,
watching it happen, like a spy,

and was casual about heights, but didn't fancy
coming down again to defy

the powers below. Odd that they didn't notice
all this climbing on the sly,

and odder still, if they knew, that they didn't ban it.
Knowing them now, you'd wonder why.

Drowning

'*Si qua mulier maritum suum, cui legitime est iuncta, dimiserit, necetur in luto*'—*Lex Burgund.*, 34, 1.

(*If any woman has killed her lawfully married husband let her be drowned in mud.*)

Death by drowning drowns the soul:
bubbles cannot carry it;
frail pops of air, farts
loosed in water are no vessels
for the immortal part of us.
And in a pit of mud, what bubbles?
There she lies, her last breath with her,
her soul rotting in her breast.

*

Is the sea better, then?
Will the salty brine preserve
pickled souls for the Day of Judgement?
Are we herrings to be trawled
in long nets by Saint Peter?
Ocean is a heavy load:
My soul flies up to thee, O God —
but not through mud, not through water.

And so, Bishop Synesius,
how can you wonder that we stand
with drawn swords on this bucking deck,
choosing to fall on friendly steel
and squirt our souls into the heavens
rather than choke them fathoms deep?

One more lash of the storm and it's done:
self-murder, but not soul-murder.

Then let the fishes feast on us
and slurp our blood after we're finished:
they'll find no souls to suck from us.
Yours, perhaps, has a safe-conduct:
you're a bishop, and subtle, and Greek.
Well, sir, pray and ponder. But our
language has no word for dilemma.
Drowning's the strongest word for death.

'Personal Poem'

It's the old story of the personal;
or of the Person—'Al', we could call him—
with his oneness, his centrality,
fingers tapping to the band music,
and his eyes glowing like that
as if he had invented the guitar;
or coming around the corner on his tractor
calling out some comment you just missed.

The radios begin at 6 a.m.
It is really a very crowded city.
You're lucky to find two rooms, one for sleeping,
and a patch of allotment for potatoes.

Here we are on the hills, and it's no better.
Of course the birds are singing, but they would.
All you get is contempt, didn't they say so?
All right, contemn us.
We asked for nothing but a few gestures—
that kiss inside his open collar,
between the neck and shoulder, shockingly
personal to watch.

It's Al again, laughing in his teeth,
telling us about his Jamaican childhood
and the time his friend had crabs
from making love to the teacher's maid.
'It gave me a funny feeling' he says
'to see them crawling there, little animals.
I hadn't even grown hair on mine.
In a way I was jealous—
imagine!' We imagine.

All these people running about in tracksuits
for nothing. And one standing at the gate
with a paper bag of bananas. 'Hi' he says,
'How are you?' Nobody answers.

29

So at the May Day rally there they are.
Surely that's his jacket she's wearing?
And the face under the hair is his,
the way she wrinkles her nose.
How people give themselves away!
Yet all we have is hearsay.

Too late to take a boat out;
and anyway, the lake's crowded,
kids and oars together, and all their voices.
But really no one in particular,
unless you say so. Unless we say so.

An Epitaph

I wish to apologize for being mangled.
It was the romantic temperament
that did for me. I could stand rejection—
so grand, 'the stone the builders rejected . . .'—
but not acceptance. 'Alas', I said
(a word I use), 'alas, I am taken
up, or in, or out of myself:
shall I never be solitary?'
Acceptance fell on me like a sandbag.
My bones crack. It squelches out of them.
Ah, acceptance! Leave me under this stone.

Being Taken from the Place

Less like an aircraft than a kettle,
this van, the way the floor buzzes
tinnily over its boiling wheels,
rolling me south.
                Sounds flick backwards
in a travelling cauldron of noise. I lie
on the metal floor, hearing their voices
whirring like mechanical flies
over the seething burr of the engine.

They won't hear if I talk to myself;
whatever I say they can't hear me.
I say 'Illness is a kind of failure.'
I say 'Northumbrian rose quartz.'

Accidents

The accidents are never happening:
they are too imaginable to be true.
The driver knows his car is still on the road,
heading for Durham in the rain.
The mother knows her baby is just asleep,
curled up with his cuddly blanket, waiting
to be lifted and fed: there's no such thing as cot-death.
The rescue party digging all night in the dunes
can't believe the tunnel has really collapsed:
the children have somehow gone to their Auntie's house;
she has lent them their cousins' pyjamas, they are sitting
giggling together in the big spare room,
pretending to try and spill each other's cocoa.

On the Land

I'm still too young to remember how
I learned to mind a team of horses,
to plough and harrow: not a knack
you'd lose easily, once you had it.

It was in the Great War, that much-
remembered age. I was a landgirl
in my puttees and boots and breeches
and a round hat like a felt halo.

We didn't mind the lads laughing:
let them while they could, we thought,
they hadn't long. But it seemed long—
hay-making, and apple-picking,

and storing all those scented things
in sneezy dimness in the barn.
Then Jack turned seventeen and went,
and I knew Ted would go soon.

He went the week of Candlemas.
After that it was all weather:
frosts and rains and spring and summer,
and the long days growing longer.

It rained for the potato harvest.
The front of my smock hung heavy
with claggy mud, from kneeling in it
mining for strays. Round segments

chopped clean off by the blade
flashed white as severed kneecaps.
I grubbed for whole ones, baby skulls
to fill my sack again and again.

When the pain came, it wouldn't
stop. I couldn't stand. I dropped
the sack and sank into a trench.
Ethel found me doubled up.

Mr Gregson took me home,
jolting on the back of the wagon.
I tossed and writhed on my hard bed,
my head hunched into the bolster,

dreaming of how if just for once,
for half an hour, the knobbly mattress
could turn into a billow of clouds
I might be able to get to sleep.

Icon

In the interests of economy
I am not going to tell you
what happened between the time
when they checked into the hotel

with its acres of tiled bathrooms
(but the bidet in theirs was cracked)
and the morning two days later
when he awoke to find her gone.

After he had read her note
and done the brief things he could do
he found himself crossing the square
to the Orthodox Cathedral.

The dark icon by the door
was patched with lumpy silver islands
nailed to the Virgin's robes; they looked
like flattened-out Monopoly tokens,

he thought: a boot, and something like
a heart, and a pair of wings, and something
oblong. They were hard to see
in the brown light, but he peered at them

for several minutes, leaning over
the scarved head of an old woman
on her knees there, blocking his view,
who prayed and prayed and wouldn't move.

Drawings

The ones not in the catalogue:
little sketches, done in her garden—this
head of a child (the same child
we saw in the picnic scene, remember?)
And trees, of course, and grasses,
and a study of hawthorn berries.
Doodles, unfinished drafts: look
at this chestnut leaf, abandoned in mid-
stroke—a telephone-call, perhaps;
a visitor; some interruption.

She may have been happier,
or happy longer, or at least more often . . .
but that's presumption. Let's move on:
grasses again; a group of stones
from her rockery, done in charcoal; and this
not quite completed pencil sketch of
a tiger lily, the springy crown
of petals curved back on itself
right to the stem, the long electric
stamens almost still vibrating.

The Telephone Call

They asked me 'Are you sitting down?
Right? This is Universal Lotteries',
they said. 'You've won the top prize,
the Ultra-super Global Special.
What would you do with a million pounds?
Or, actually, with more than a million—
not that it makes a lot of difference
once you're a millionaire.' And they laughed.

'Are you OK?' they asked—'Still there?
Come on, now, tell us, how does it feel?'
I said 'I just . . . I can't believe it!'
They said 'That's what they all say.
What else? Go on, tell us about it.'
I said 'I feel the top of my head
has floated off, out through the window,
revolving like a flying saucer.'

'That's unusual' they said. 'Go on.'
I said 'I'm finding it hard to talk.
My throat's gone dry, my nose is tingling.
I think I'm going to sneeze—or cry.'
'That's right' they said, 'don't be ashamed
of giving way to your emotions.
It isn't every day you hear
you're going to get a million pounds.

Relax, now, have a little cry;
we'll give you a moment . . .' 'Hang on!' I said.
'I haven't bought a lottery ticket
for years and years. And what did you say
the company's called?' They laughed again.
'Not to worry about a ticket.
We're Universal. We operate
a Retrospective Chances Module.

Nearly everyone's bought a ticket
in some lottery or another,
once at least. We buy up the files,
feed the names into our computer,
and see who the lucky person is.'
'Well, that's incredible' I said.
'It's marvellous. I still can't quite . . .
I'll believe it when I see the cheque.'

'Oh,' they said, 'there's no cheque.'
'But the money?' 'We don't deal in money.
Experiences are what we deal in.
You've had a great experience, right?
Exciting? Something you'll remember?
That's your prize. So congratulations
from all of us at Universal.
Have a nice day!' And the line went dead.

INCIDENTALS

Excavations

Here is a hole full of men shouting
'I don't love you. I loved you once
but I don't now. I went off you,
or I was frightened, or my wife was pregnant,
or I found I preferred men instead.'

What can I say to that kind of talk?
'Thank you for being honest, you
who were so shifty when it happened,
pretending you were suddenly busy
with your new job or your new conscience.'

I chuck them a shovelful of earth
to make them blink for a bit, to smirch
their green eyes and their long lashes
or their brown eyes . . . Pretty bastards:
the rain will wash their bawling faces

and I bear them little enough ill will.
Now on to the next hole,
covered and fairly well stamped down,
full of the men whom I stopped loving
and didn't always tell at the time—

being, I found, rather busy
with my new man or my new freedom.
These are quiet and unaccusing,
cuddled up with their subsequent ladies,
hardly unsettling the bumpy ground.

Pastoral

Eat their own hair, sheep do,
nibbling away under the snow, under their bellies—
calling it wool makes it no more palatable.

What else is there to do in the big drifts,
forced against a wall of wet stone?
But let me have your hair to nibble

before we are in winter; and the thong
of dark seeds you wear at your neck;
and for my tongue the salt on your skin to gobble.

Kissing

The young are walking on the riverbank,
arms around each other's waists and shoulders,
pretending to be looking at the waterlilies
and what might be a nest of some kind, over
there, which two who are clamped together
mouth to mouth have forgotten about.
The others, making courteous detours
around them, talk, stop talking, kiss.
They can see no one older than themselves.
It's their river. They've got all day.

Seeing's not everything. At this very
moment the middle-aged are kissing
in the backs of taxis, on the way
to airports and stations. Their mouths and tongues
are soft and powerful and as moist as ever.
Their hands are not inside each other's clothes
(because of the driver) but locked so tightly
together that it hurts: it may leave marks
on their not of course youthful skin, which they won't
notice. They too may have futures.

Double-Take

You see your next-door neighbour from above,
from an upstairs window, and he reminds you
of your ex-lover, who is bald on top,
which you had forgotten. At ground level
there is no resemblance. Next time you chat
with your next-door neighbour, you are relieved
to find that you don't fancy him.

A week later you meet your ex-lover
at a party, after more than a year.
He reminds you (although only slightly)
of your next-door neighbour. He has a paunch
like your neighbour's before he went cn that diet.
You remember how much you despise him.

He behaves as if he's pleased to see you.
When you leave (a little earlier
than you'd intended, to get away)
he gives you a kiss which is more than neighbourly
and says he'll ring you. He seems to mean it.
How odd! But you are quite relieved
to find that you don't fancy him.

Unless you do? Or why that sudden
something, once you get outside
in the air? Why are your legs prancing
so cheerfully along the pavement?
And what exactly have you just remembered?
You go home cursing chemistry.

Choices

There was never just one book for the desert island,
one perfectly tissue-typed aesthetic match,
that wouldn't drive you crazy within six months;
just as there was never one all-purpose
ideal outfit, unquestionably right
for wearing at the ball on the Titanic
and also in the lifeboat afterwards.

And never, *a fortiori*, just one man;
if it's not their conversation or their habits
(more irritating, even, than your own—
and who would you wish those on?) it's their bodies:
two-thirds of them get fatter by the minute,
the bony ones turn out to be psychopaths,
and the few in the middle range go bald.

Somehow you'll end up there, on the island,
in your old jeans and that comic dressing-gown
one of the fast-fatteners always laughed at,
with a blank notebook (all you've brought to read)
and a sea-and-sun-proof crate of cigarettes;
but with nobody, thank God, to lecture you
on how he managed to give them up.

THATCHERLAND

Street Scene, London N2

This is the front door. You can just see
the number on it, there behind the piano,
between the young man with the fierce expression
and the one with the axe, who's trying not to laugh.

Those furry-headed plants beside the step
are Michaelmas daisies, as perhaps you've guessed,
although they're not in colour; and the path
is tiled in red and black, like a Dutch interior.

But the photograph, of course, is black and white.
The piano also sported black and white
when it was whole (look, you can see its ribcage,
the wiry harp inside it, a spread wing.)

The young men are playing Laurel and Hardy
(though both are tall, and neither of them is fat,
and one of them is actually a pianist):
they are committing a pianocide.

It wasn't really much of a piano:
warped and fungoid, grossly out of tune—
facts they have not imparted to the wincing
passers-by, whom you will have to imagine.

You will also have to imagine, if you dare,
the jangling chords of axe-blow, saw-stroke, screeching
timber, wires twanged in a terminal
appassionato. This is a silent picture.

Laurel and Hardy will complete their show:
the wires, released from their frame, will thrash and tangle
and be tamed into a ball; the varnished panels
will be sawn stacks of boards and blocks and kindling.

Later the mother will come home for Christmas.
The fire will purr and tinkle in the grate,
a chromatic harmony of tones; and somewhere
there'll be a muffled sack of snarling keys.

Gentlemen's Hairdressers

The barbers' shop has gone anonymous:
white paint, glossy as Brilliantine
('The Perfect Hairdressing') has covered
Jim's and Alfred's friendly monickers.

GENTLEMENS HAIRD in chaste blue Roman
glorifies pure form. The man
on the ladder lays a scarlet slash
of marking-tape for the next upright.

Below him Jim and Alfred are still
in business. Alfred munches a pie
and dusts the crumbs from his grey moustache
over the racing-page. A gentleman

tilts his head under Jim's clippers.
In the window the Durex poster,
the one with the motorbike, has faded
to pale northern shades of sea.

An hour later the ladder's gone
and purity's been deposed: the lettering's
denser now, the Roman caps
blocked in with three-dimensional grey.

The word 'Styling' in shapeless cursive
wriggles above the open door.
Swaddled and perched on Alfred's chair
a tiny Greek boy squeals and squeals.

Post Office

The queue's right out through the glass doors
to the street: Thursday, pension day.
They built this Post Office too small.
Of course, the previous one was smaller—
a tiny prefab, next to the betting-shop,
says the man who's just arrived;
and the present one, at which we're queuing,
was cherry-trees in front of a church.
The church was where the supermarket is:
'My wife and I got married in that church'
the man says. 'We hold hands sometimes
when we're standing waiting at the checkout—
have a little moment together!' He laughs.
The queue shuffles forward a step.
Three members of it silently vow
never to grow old in this suburb;
one vows never to grow old at all.
'I first met her over there' the man says,
'on that corner where the bank is now.
The other corner was Williams Brothers—
remember Williams Brothers? They gave you tokens,
tin money, like, for your dividend.'
The woman in front of him remembers.
She nods, and swivels her loose lower denture,
remembering Williams Brothers' metal tokens,
and the marble slab on the cheese-counter,
and the carved mahogany booth where you went to pay.
The boy in front of her is chewing gum;
his jaws rotate with the same motion
as hers: to and fro, to and fro.

Demonstration

'YOU ARE NOW WALKING IN THE ROAD.
The lines marked out with sticky tape
are where the kerb is going to be
under the traffic-scheme proposals.
This tree will go. The flower-beds
and seats outside the supermarket
will go. The pavements will be narrowed
to make room for six lanes of traffic.'

We are now walking in the road
with a few banners and some leaflets
and forms to sign for a petition.
The Council will ignore them all.
The Council wants a monster junction
with traffic-islands, metal railings,
computer-managed lights and crossings,
and lots and lots of lanes of traffic.

We are still walking in the road.
It seems a long time since we started,
and most of us are getting older
(the ones who aren't, of course, are dead.)
This borough has the highest number
of pensioners in Greater London.
Perhaps the junction, with its modern
split-second lights, will cut them down.

But while we're walking in the road
others are driving. At our backs
we hear the roar of heavy traffic
churning from Finchley to Westminster;
and over it, from a loudspeaker,
a stern, conceited female voice
with artificial vowels exhorts us:
'Come with us into the nineties!'

Witnesses

We three in our dark decent clothes,
unlike ourselves, more like the three
witches, we say, crouched over the only
ashtray, smoke floating into our hair,

wait. An hour; another hour.
If you stand up and walk ten steps
to the glass doors you can see her there
in the witness box, a Joan of Arc,

straight, still, her neck slender,
her lips moving from time to time
in reply to voices we can't hear:
'I put it to you . . . I should like to suggest . . .'

It's her small child who is at stake.
His future hangs from these black-clad
proceedings, these ferretings under her sober
dress, under our skirts and dresses

to sniff out corruption: 'I put it to you
that in fact your husband . . . that my client . . .
that you yourself initiated the violence . . .
that your hysteria . . .' She sits like marble.

We pace the corridors, peep at the distance
from door to witness box (two steps up,
remember, be careful not to trip
when the time comes) and imagine them there,

the ones we can't see. A man in a wig
and black robes. Two other men
in lesser wigs and gowns. More men
in dark suits. We sit down together,

shake the smoke from our hair, pass round
more cigarettes (to be held carefully
so as not to smirch our own meek versions
of their clothing), and wait to be called.

Last Song

Goodbye, sweet symmetry. Goodbye, sweet world
of mirror-images and matching halves,
where animals have usually four legs
and people nearly always two;
where birds and bats and butterflies and bees
have balanced wings, and even flies
can fly straight if they try. Goodbye
to one-a-side for eyes and ears and arms
and breasts and balls and shoulder-blades
and hands; goodbye to the straight line
drawn down the central spine,
making us double in a world
where oddness is acceptable only
under the sea, for the lop-sided lobster,
the wonky oyster, the creepily rotated
flatfish with both eyes over one gill;
goodbye to the sweet certitudes of our
mammalian order, where to be
born with one eye or three thumbs
points to not being human. It will come.

In the next world, when this one's gone skew-whiff,
we shall be algae or lichen, things
we've hardly even needed to pronounce.
If the flounder still exists it will be king.